D1103905

Patrick Henry

written and illustrated by
Rod Espinosa

magic
Wagon

visit us at
www.abdopublishing.com

Published by Magic Wagon, a division of the ABDO Publishing Group, 8000 West 78th Street, Edina, Minnesota 55439. Copyright © 2008 by Abdo Consulting Group, Inc. International copyrights reserved in all countries. All rights reserved. No part of this book may be reproduced in any form without written permission from the publisher. Graphic Planet™ is a trademark and logo of Magic Wagon.

Printed in the United States.

Written and illustrated by Rod Espinosa
Colored and lettered by Rod Espinosa
Edited by Stephanie Hedlund
Interior layout and design by Antarctic Press
Cover art by Rod Espinosa
Cover design by Neil Klinepier

Library of Congress Cataloging-in-Publication Data

Espinosa, Rod.
   Patrick Henry / written and illustrated by Rod Espinosa.
   p. cm. -- (Bio-graphics)
   Includes bibliographical references and index.
   ISBN-13: 978-1-60270-070-3
1. Henry, Patrick, 1736-1799--Juvenile literature. 2. Legislators--United States--Biography--Juvenile literature. 3. United States. Continental Congress--Biography--Juvenile literature. 4. Virginia--Politics and government--1775-1783--Juvenile literature. 5. United States--Politics and government--1775-1783--Juvenile literature. 6. Graphic novels. I. Title.

 E302.6.H5E85 2008
 973.3092--dc22
 [B]   2007012711

TABLE of CONTENTS

"Give me liberty…or give me death…"
These are the immortal words of one man: Patrick Henry.
He was one of the Founding Fathers of the United States of America…
a man who valued freedom and wanted freedom for others.

What led to this famous declaration?
What circumstances led him to revolt against England?
To learn about these things, we have to go back…
to a time when his home state of Virginia, just like the other states,
was a colony of the British Empire…

Chapter 1 — Farm Boy Beginning

Patrick Henry was born on May 29, 1736, to John and Sarah Syme Henry.

They were plantation owners. John was educated in Scotland before coming to America. There, he met Sarah.

They lived on a farm called Studley.

Young Patrick went to school on and off until he was 10. The rest of the time, he helped on the family farm. Tobacco was the chief product of Virginia in those days.

DO YOU MEAN THIS TINY SEEDLING WILL GROW INTO THOSE LARGE PLANTS?

YES, IT WILL, PATRICK.

John eventually decided to teach his son himself. Patrick was taught mathematics, Greek, and Latin by his father. He loved his father.

FATHER, WHO INVENTED MATH?

MATH WAS DEVELOPED BY MEN LIKE PYTHAGORAS AND ARCHIMEDES.

Although Patrick was a smart kid, he did not relish studying. He loved the outdoors. Fishing and exploring the woods were his favorite pastimes. He learned to play the violin and flute after he broke his collarbone.

Eight daughters and another son were born after Patrick. The happy Henry home also included John Syme, Jr., Sarah's son from a previous marriage.

Although they were wealthy planters, the Henrys lived a simpler life. Instead of fancy clothes, baubles, and jewels, they bought books. They treasured knowledge above all else.

When Patrick turned 14, his father sent him to work in a country store to learn a trade.

When he turned 16, his father bought him a store to run. It didn't do well, and by the time he turned 19, it was failing.

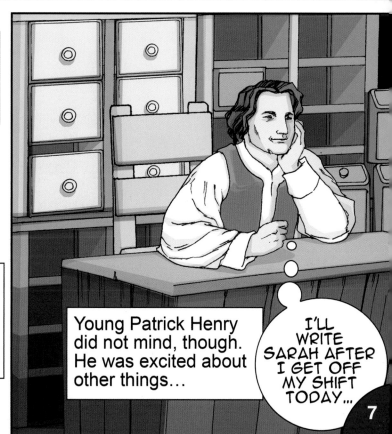

Young Patrick Henry did not mind, though. He was excited about other things…

I'LL WRITE SARAH AFTER I GET OFF MY SHIFT TODAY…

7

Patrick Henry married 16-year-old Sarah Shelton. For a dowry, Sarah's father gave the couple 300 acres to farm for their own. Along with the plantation came six slaves.

HERE WE ARE, MY LOVE. PINE SLASH. MY FATHER LIKED THIS PLACE.

IT WAS REALLY NICE OF YOUR FATHER TO GIVE US THIS FARM.

Patrick worked hard to make Pine Slash profitable. He even worked alongside his slaves.

A fire destroyed their farm. Henry sold the slaves to raise money to open another store. Soon, Patrick and Sarah had a child.

I HOPE THIS WILL BE A NEW START FOR US.

But 1759 was a bad year for tobacco, and many plantation owners were ruined. France and Britain were at war. Many of Henry's friends went off and fought in what was eventually known as the French and Indian War.

England taxed the colonies to pay for this new war.

Henry's new store did not do well...

PEOPLE JUST DON'T HAVE MONEY TO BUY GOODS.

WHAT CAN WE DO? THEIR MONEY IS USED UP PAYING FOR TAXES FOR THE WARS OF THE CROWN.

With the French and Indian War going on, Patrick Henry continued to struggle with his store. He finally went out of business in 1759. For a while, he entertained at parties with his flute and fiddle. At one gathering, he met a young man named Thomas Jefferson.

TOM, WHAT DO YOU THINK ABOUT YOUNG HENRY THERE?

HIS MANNERS HAVE SOMETHING OF COARSENESS IN THEM. HIS PASSION SEEMS TO BE MUSIC, DANCING, AND PLEASURE.

Henry still needed to support his family. He considered being a teacher or a minister, but those required years of study and plenty of money.

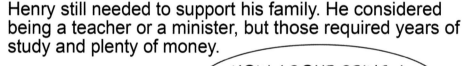

HOW ABOUT BEING A LAWYER? I THINK I MIGHT BE GOOD AT ARGUING CASES.

YOU DO LIKE TALKING. YOU SHOULD SEE YOUR UNCLE ABOUT ATTENDING COURT IN HANOVER.

The Henrys moved into a room in the Hanover tavern run by Sarah's father. Across from the inn was the courthouse.

Six of the 12 justices were Patrick's relatives. He sat in the courtroom and listened often. He could only afford to buy two law books. In April 1760, he was tested by the colony's finest lawyers.

THANK YOU. I WILL.

CONGRATULATIONS! YOUR KNOWLEDGE OF LAW IS A BIT LACKING, BUT WE WERE IMPRESSED WITH YOUR ABILITY TO ARGUE CASES CONVINCINGLY.

STUDY HARD TO EARN YOUR NEW TITLE.

And so Patrick Henry became a lawyer in 1760. Given the license to practice law, he worked hard. He argued several cases for his relatives.

HAVE THEY BEGUN YET?

THEY JUST SAT DOWN AFTER THE MORNING PRAYERS! HURRY, THIS WAY!

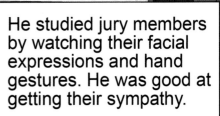

He studied jury members by watching their facial expressions and hand gestures. He was good at getting their sympathy.

Henry argued a total of 1,185 cases in just three short years. By 1764, he was doing really well.

THANK YOU, SIR... IF IT WERE NOT FOR YOU, THE PROPRIETORS SURELY WOULD HAVE GOTTEN MY FARM!

LET ME KNOW IF THIS HAPPENS AGAIN TO ANYONE YOU KNOW.

PEOPLE SHOULD NOT BE TRICKED INTO GIVING UP THEIR PROPERTY BY THOSE WHO INTERPRET CERTAIN LAWS TO THEIR ENDS.

Henry began purchasing land. The family moved often, for they needed more and more room as more children were born.

Patrick and Sarah had three sons and three daughters. Henry was well established throughout Virginia by the time their last child was born. Their huge household even included Henry's brothers and sisters.

At the Henry household, there was plenty of singing, books, and laughter.

Henry would ride his horse as far as 100 miles to a hearing. At other times, he would walk 15 miles to work. He never turned down a request for help. All his family was proud of him.

Soon, he was able to lend his father some money. By 1767, he was lending money to Sarah's father.

...CHURCH MINISTERS MAKING A LOT OF MONEY TAXING SUFFERING TOBACCO FARMERS? ...AND YOU SAY THEY ARE ARGUING THIS CASE IN VIRGINIA'S LEGISLATURE?

YES, I THOUGHT YOU SHOULD KNOW ABOUT IT.

I SHALL DEPART WITH ALL SPEED.

13

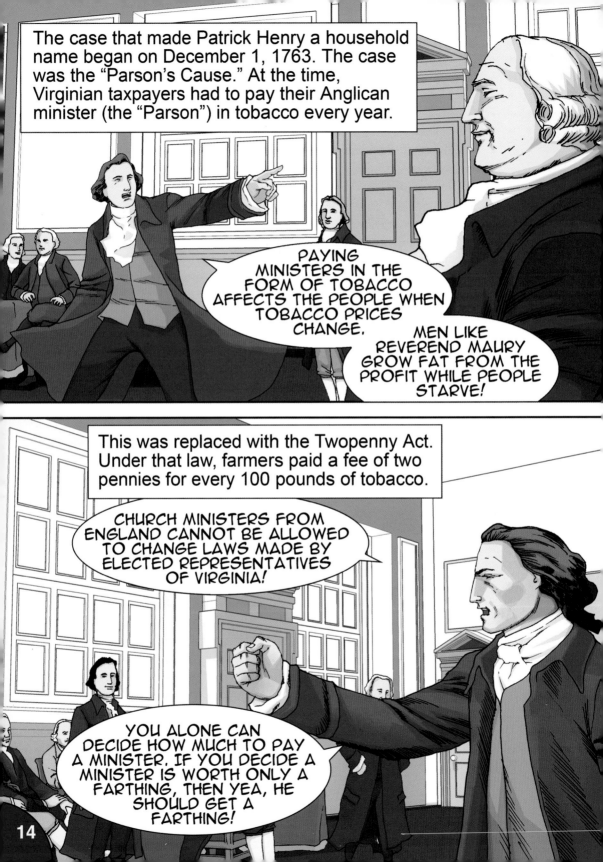

The case that made Patrick Henry a household name began on December 1, 1763. The case was the "Parson's Cause." At the time, Virginian taxpayers had to pay their Anglican minister (the "Parson") in tobacco every year.

PAYING MINISTERS IN THE FORM OF TOBACCO AFFECTS THE PEOPLE WHEN TOBACCO PRICES CHANGE.

MEN LIKE REVEREND MAURY GROW FAT FROM THE PROFIT WHILE PEOPLE STARVE!

This was replaced with the Twopenny Act. Under that law, farmers paid a fee of two pennies for every 100 pounds of tobacco.

CHURCH MINISTERS FROM ENGLAND CANNOT BE ALLOWED TO CHANGE LAWS MADE BY ELECTED REPRESENTATIVES OF VIRGINIA!

YOU ALONE CAN DECIDE HOW MUCH TO PAY A MINISTER. IF YOU DECIDE A MINISTER IS WORTH ONLY A FARTHING, THEN YEA, HE SHOULD GET A FARTHING!

In less than five minutes, the jury returned with a verdict of:

ONE FARTHING FOR REVEREND MAURY!

HURRAH FOR PATRICK HENRY!

In 1765, Patrick Henry was elected to Virginia's House of Burgesses.

The plainly dressed 29-year-old lawyer was ignored by the wealthy delegates.

On his first day at the assembly, they were complaining about a new tax handed to them by the English Parliament.

This was the Stamp Act of 1765. It was a tax on every piece of printed matter in the colonies. Books, newspapers, legal papers, and even playing cards were included.

THE KING OF ENGLAND CANNOT TAX US LIKE THIS! THIS IS AN ACT OF TYRANNY!

TREASON! TREASON!

IF THIS BE TREASON, MAKE THE MOST OF IT!

Virginia's legislature passed Henry's motion to end the Stamp Act.

Henry was elected again and again to the House of Burgesses. He would be a busy man for the next decade. At home, however, Sarah's health began to fail after the birth of their sixth child.

By 1772, Sarah had to be fed her meals and watched all the time. It was a sad time for Henry and his family.

FATHER... I'M SCARED... WHEN WILL MOMMA BE BETTER?

WE'RE ALL HOPING SOON, MY LOVE.

Henry kept working. He turned his attention to the issue of freedom of religion. He accepted cases where he had to defend Baptists or Presbyterian ministers who had been jailed for practicing their religion.

PEOPLE SHOULD BE FREE TO PRACTICE WHATEVER FAITH THEY WANT.

A new royal governor was appointed in 1773. Lord Dunsmore was the new royal governor of Virginia. He closed the House of Burgesses several times so Henry and the lawmakers could not stir up more trouble for the crown.

THIS LEGISLATURE IS NOW CLOSED! THERE SHALL BE NO ILLEGAL GATHERINGS HERE OR AT ANY OTHER PLACE.

THOSE CAUGHT GATHERING ILLEGALLY SHALL BE PUNISHED BY HIS MAJESTY'S COURT!

Despite the king's orders, Henry and his allies met secretly in a nearby tavern.

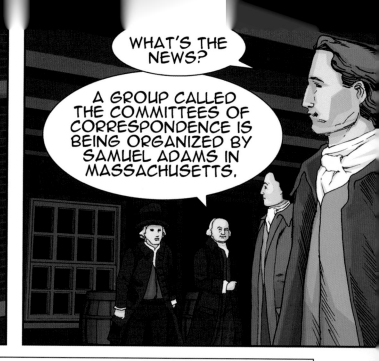

WHAT'S THE NEWS?

A GROUP CALLED THE COMMITTEES OF CORRESPONDENCE IS BEING ORGANIZED BY SAMUEL ADAMS IN MASSACHUSETTS.

The English Parliament repealed the Stamp Act. But they replaced it with a new set of taxes. The Townshend Act taxed paint, glass, paper, and tea imported from Britain.

The tea taxes especially upset Americans. They decided to boycott British tea.

On December 16, 1773, the people of Boston rallied to action. They boarded a ship full of tea crates and tossed the crates into the sea!

The event was known as the Boston Tea Party.

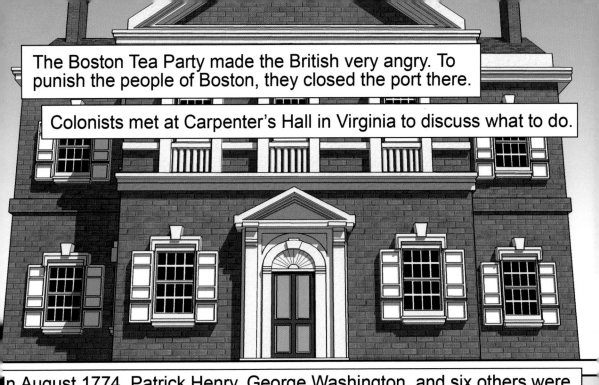

The Boston Tea Party made the British very angry. To punish the people of Boston, they closed the port there.

Colonists met at Carpenter's Hall in Virginia to discuss what to do.

In August 1774, Patrick Henry, George Washington, and six others were elected to represent Virginia. They were to attend the First Continental Congress. If they were discovered, they could be arrested for treason.

During the Continental Congress, Henry urged the colonies to work together. To unite under one banner was a unique idea back then.

IF WE SUCCEED, WE WILL NOT BE KNOWN AS VIRGINIANS, PENNSYLVANIANS, OR NEW YORKERS... WE WILL BE KNOWN AS AMERICANS!

ONWARD THEN... TO PHILADELPHIA!

At this time, Patrick's loving wife Sarah died.

Chapter 4 Give Me Liberty or Give Me Death!

Lord Dunsmore ordered the arrest of Henry and other Virginian leaders. At a meeting in Richmond in 1775, Henry gave a speech that is remembered to this day.

THE WAR IS INEVITABLE, AND LET IT COME. I REPEAT... LET IT COME!

I KNOW NOT WHAT COURSE OTHERS MAY TAKE; BUT AS FOR ME... GIVE ME LIBERTY OR GIVE ME DEATH!

The delegates including Thomas Jefferson agreed with Henry. He was appointed to a committee to make plans.

THOSE WERE BRAVE WORDS YOU SAID IN THERE, PATRICK.

THERE'S NO TURNING BACK NOW, THOMAS...

INDEED. ONWARD TO FREEDOM!

Henry went to Hanover and assembled a volunteer militia. The English got nervous.

They ordered all gunpowder in the colonies confiscated.

CONFOUND IT! FIGHTING HAS BEGUN IN LEXINGTON AND CONCORD. WE NEED TO--

MY LORD, LOO THERE!

WHAT!? THEY'RE COMING TOWARDS US!

In Virginia, Lord Dunsmore's English marines secretly took the militia's gunpowder in the middle of the night.

On May 2, 1775, several hundred volunteers led by Henry marched on the governor's mansion. They demanded the return of their gunpowder.

Lord Dunsmore was so panicked he even gave rifles to his slaves. English soldiers placed cannons around the mansion.

The Second Continental Congress met again in 1775. George Washington was elected commander-in-chief of the Continental army then based in Boston.

WE WOULD RATHER DIE FREE MEN THAN LIVE AS SLAVES.

WE MUST BEGIN DRAFTING A RESOLUTION FOR INDEPENDENCE.

IF WE SUCCEED, WE WILL HAVE A NEW NATION.

Henry was chosen to lead the Virginia militia. When people found out he was the commander, enlistments increased dramatically.

THE BRITISH ARE COMING!

SECURE THE TOWN!

On June 29, 1776, Patrick Henry was elected governor of Virginia.

On July 4, the Second Continental Congress approved the Declaration of Independence. During his second one-year term as governor, Henry met Dorothea Dandridge.

CHILDREN, YOU REMEMBER AUNT DOROTHEA, DON'T YOU? SHE'S GOING TO BE YOUR NEW MOTHER.

GOOD AFTERNOON, MA'AM!

Dorothea's grandfather was once governor of Virginia. She was also the cousin of George Washington's wife, Martha. They married on October 9, 1777.

The Continental army led by Washington lost many battles. Many people lost faith, but Henry remained loyal to Washington throughout. During the winter of 1777, Washington's men were starving and freezing at Valley Forge, Pennsylvania. Henry worked frantically to supply food and clothing to the soldiers.

LISTEN TO ME!

OUR SOLDIERS ARE FREEZING OUT THERE WHILE WE'RE WARM AND COZY IN OUR HOMES! THEY NEED SHELTER AND FOOD NOW!

After years of service as governor, Henry was succeeded by Thomas Jefferson. The British forces were spreading everywhere. There were not enough Continentals to stop them. Henry and Jefferson barely escaped arrest.

WE ARE HERE FOR PATRICK HENRY AND THOMAS JEFFERSON. ARE THEY INSIDE?

I HAVEN'T SEEN MY HUSBAND IN HALF A YEAR, SIR.

In 1780, Henry was elected to the Virginia House. The next year, Washington, aided by the French, defeated the British army at Yorktown.

PATRICK, DOROTHEA! HAVE YOU HEARD? CORNWALLIS HAS SURRENDERED AT YORKTOWN!

THEY DID IT! WE WON!

Soon after, the U.S. Constitution was ratified. Henry contributed by suggesting they add a bill of rights.

25

Henry was offered the job of American ambassador to Spain, secretary of state, or chief justice of the Supreme Court. George Washington wanted him to take on any of these jobs. But Henry was interested only in one thing: working as a lawyer in Virginia.

He continued to help people. He bought and sold land, becoming one of the largest landholders in Virginia. He had a huge family to support—six children from Sarah and 11 children with Dorothea.

And just like his father's, Patrick's family lived simply and valued books and knowledge.

In 1799, Henry was again elected to the Virginia House, but he was too ill to take office. He died at home in the presence of his loved ones on June 6, 1799. He was 63.

THE AMERICAN COLONIES IN 1775

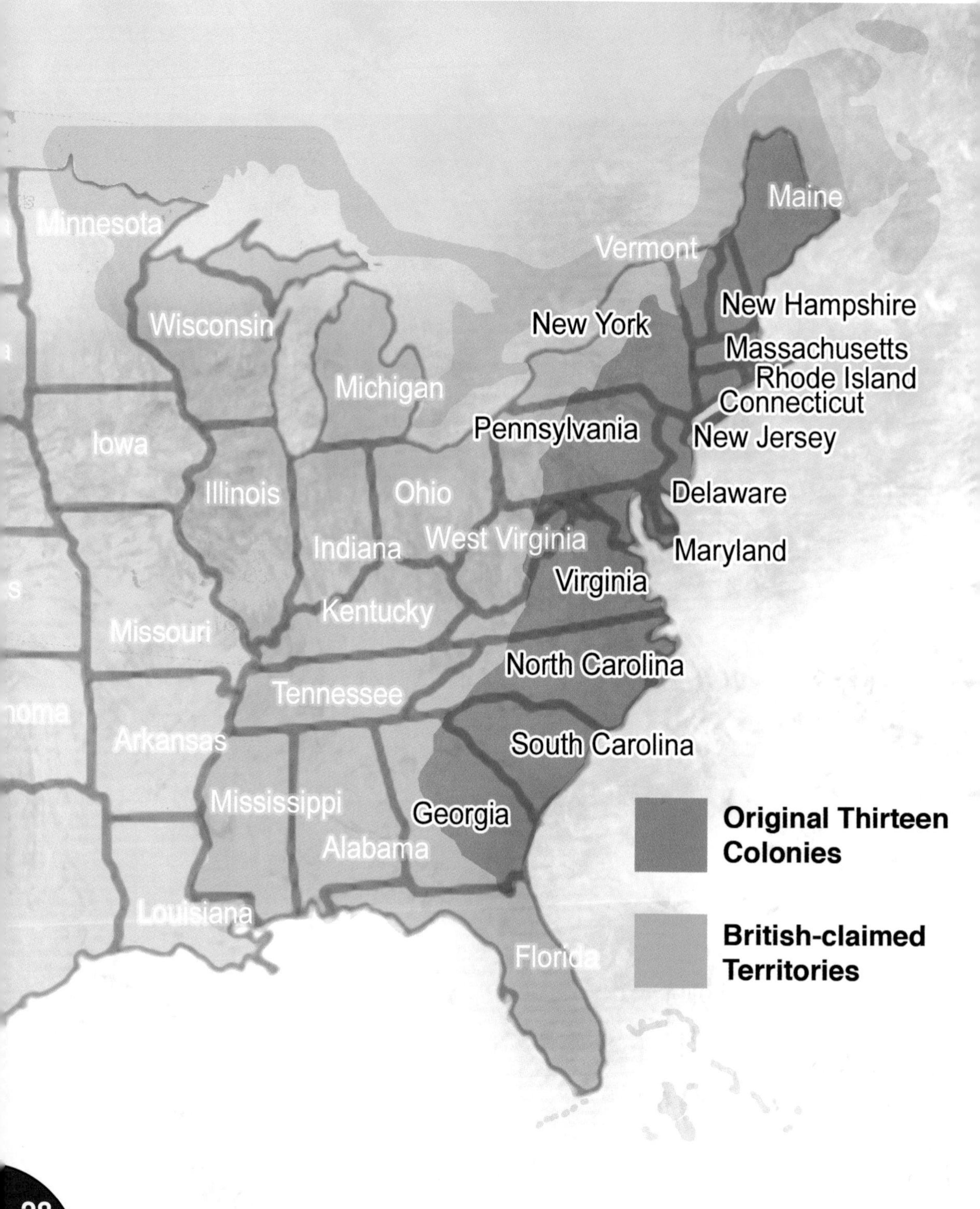
Minnesota
Wisconsin
Michigan
Iowa
Illinois
Indiana
Ohio
West Virginia
Kentucky
Missouri
Tennessee
Arkansas
Mississippi
Alabama
Louisiana
Florida
Maine
Vermont
New York
New Hampshire
Massachusetts
Rhode Island
Connecticut
Pennsylvania
New Jersey
Delaware
Maryland
Virginia
North Carolina
South Carolina
Georgia
Original Thirteen Colonies
British-claimed Territories

Timeline

May 29, 1736 - Patrick Henry was born to John and Sarah Winston Henry.

1754 - The French and Indian War began. Patrick married Sarah Shelton.

April 15, 1760 - Henry was presented with a law license to the court of Goochland County.

December 1, 1763 - Henry criticized the king for disallowing a statute.

May 1765 - Henry was elected to the House of Burgesses from Louisa County. He gave resolutions against the Stamp Act, which helped start the Revolution.

1772 - Henry took over the law practice of Robert Carter Nicholas and became a member of Virginia's Committee of Correspondence.

August 1774 - Henry was elected to the First Continental Congress.

March 23, 1775 - Henry gave his famous "Liberty or Death" speech.

April 19, 1775 - The American Revolutionary War began.

June 29, 1776 - Henry was elected the first governor of the commonwealth of Virginia.

October 19, 1781 - The British surrendered at Yorktown, ending the war.

1783 - Henry established Hampden Sydney College.

March 1788 - Henry was elected to the Virginia House of Delegates and over the year helped shape the Bill of Rights of the Constitution.

June 6, 1799 - Patrick Henry died at age 63.

Further Reading

Grote, JoAnn A. *Patrick Henry.* New York: Facts on File, Inc., 1999.

Heinrichs, Ann. *Patrick Henry.* Mankato: The Child's World, Inc., 2004.

Kallen, Stuart A. *Patrick Henry.* Founding Fathers. Edina: ABDO Publishing Company, 2001.

McPherson, Stephanie Sammartino. *Liberty or Death: A Story about Patrick Henry.* Minneapolis: Lerner Publishing Group, 2003.

Glossary

confiscate - to seize by authority.

Declaration of Independence - an essay written at the Second Continental Congress in 1776, announcing the separation of the American colonies from England.

Founding Fathers - the men who attended the Constitutional Convention in Philadelphia, Pennsylvania, in 1787. They helped write the U.S. Constitution.

immortal - something that will live or be remembered always.

ratify - to officially approve.

tyranny - a government where one person has absolute power. The person in power is called a tyrant.

unique - being the only one of its kind.

Web Sites

To learn more about Patrick Henry, visit ABDO Publishing Company on the World Wide Web at **www.abdopublishing.com.** Web sites about Henry are featured on our Book Links page. These links are routinely monitored and updated to provide the most current information available.

Index

7/4)